Needlepoint Designs
from American Indian Art

Needlepoint Designs from American Indian Art

Nora Cammann

photographs and illustrations
by Rolf Siljander

CHARLES SCRIBNER'S SONS • NEW YORK

For Freddy, Peter and Philip,

with thanks for your understanding,

encouragement, and patience.

Acknowledgments

Thanks and gratitude are inadequate as *none* of this book would have been possible without the help and generosity of the following people:

Stanley A. Freed, Ph.D., Chairman of the Department of Anthropology and Curator of North American Ethnology, The American Museum of Natural History;

Gardner D. Stout, President, The American Museum of Natural History;

Mr. and Mrs. Michael Gaccino, Gaccino Decorators;

Wendy Johnson and Patricia Chaarte, 2 Needles, A Needlepoint Design Studio.

Contents

Needlepoint Designs
from American Indian Art

Introduction

For over a year I have been doing odd jobs at The American Museum of Natural History in New York. In walking through the halls of the Museum I was overwhelmed with the wealth of designs available to the needlework aficionado. These designs are accessible to everyone going through the galleries.

As an odd-jobber at the Museum, I have been given access to the storerooms—they are full of glorious pieces. All of the designs in this book are from the storerooms. Thus, in addition to the designs, you will get a behind-the-scenes peek at the Museum collection.

I feel it is interesting to know a little about the peoples who created these lively designs. Therefore, while trying not to be pedantic, I will give you a bit of background with each group of designs.

The designs are simple. Transposing the designs from one medium to another was fascinating. In some cases, such as the bargello-like bag on page 64, the transposition is exact —that is, the original design and color are perfect "as is." In other cases, such as the quail and the fish pillows on pages 21, 25, the design is so simple that something had to be added. In this case elaborate stitches were used to enhance the design.

The process of discovering what each design needs and how to do it is, to me, the joy of this sort of needlework. Each of us sees things differently and has a different sense of color and balance. Therefore, I encourage you to have

2

a good time—look at the design, look at the photographs, and then do your own adapting. You will probably have to rip and re-do and rip and re-do, but the finished piece will be yours alone.

If you decide to change the colors, I strongly suggest that you color the design with crayons or colored pencils before you start. Color changes can completely change the balance of a design, so look at it before you start to stitch.

Whether you decide to follow the instructions or change the designs to suit your fancy, the primary consideration is to *enjoy* what you do. Choose a design you really like and colors that please you—and *have fun*!

How

Canvas

Canvas is made in two kinds of mesh. I prefer to use penelope canvas when mixing crewel and needlepoint stitches. The penelope canvas, with its double threads and double holes, acts more like fabric, providing more places to insert the needle and more threads to hold the stitches in place. Thus, you may fill in the background better as the "half steps" in the canvas will hold the background stitch snug against the crewel stitches.

Just a note on backgrounds while we're here. Whenever you use the regular background stitch please use the basket-weave stitch. It makes a much stronger and much smoother job. Also, it will not pull the canvas as much when you are working.

Mono

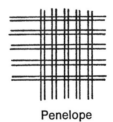

Penelope

Size

Many of the designs are drawn on ten-point graph paper. If you use ten-point canvas the design will be the same size as the graph-paper pattern. If you wish a larger or smaller finished piece, you may use coarser or finer canvas, you may regulate the area of the background, or you may change the border. If you change the dimensions by using different size canvas all the proportions will remain constant.

4

For example, although the turtle pattern on page 18 is on ten-point graph paper, the cushion is worked on five-point canvas, but the proportions remain the same. However, if you change the dimensions by varying the stitch count of the background or the border, you must recount and re-proportion the border design. Don't be scared off—it's not difficult.

For example, if you are using the scroll border, shorten or lengthen the center of the scroll.

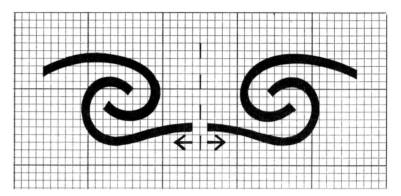

If you are using the Z border, use more or less vertical lines between the Z areas.

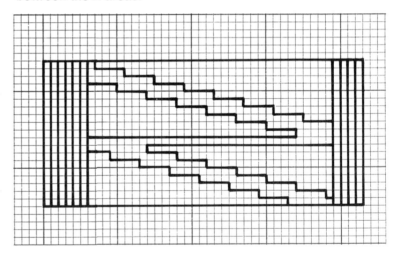

If you are using the rectangular border, rearrange the position of the individual areas as described on page 42. Easiest of all, change the border to a simple linear border—many of the earlier pieces have only three or four simple lines as borders.

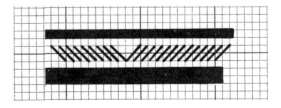

Making Your Own Borders

I have used three kinds of borders: round, square, and boxed. In many of the designs more than one border design is shown. However, you may want to use one not illustrated, so let me give you a few ideas on adapting borders.

With a simple line border there is no problem whatever, but any other pattern must be reworked to the shape of the border. Let me show you what I mean by outlining the planning of the border of the turtle cushion on page 20.

The original border is a lovely design, perfect for a round border, but troublesome for a square border because it is a directional pattern.

Thus, when we force it to go at right angles, the pattern no longer matches—the scroll will not curve around the corner.

Spacing a directional border for a corner will make it fit, but the corner design will be asymmetrical.

On a square border the pattern must be made to meet the corner the same way from both sides.

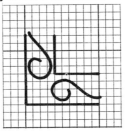

The easiest way to accomplish this is to reverse one half of the pattern. To do this, find the center of your border and

6

lay out half of the pattern. Then trace it on tracing paper.

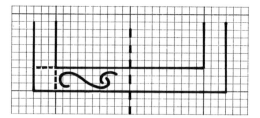

Now, turn the tracing paper over so the pattern is reversed. Lay this out the same way you did the first half, but on the other end of the border. Now, join the two halves and you will have a continuous, balanced border.

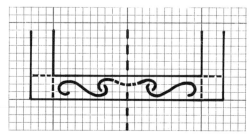

The transitional corner design must be filled in. Try to take a shape from the central design for the corner. In the case of the turtle there are two possibilities.

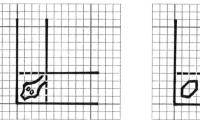 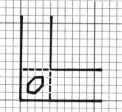

The turtle head   The shell

The boxed border is handled without the corner design.

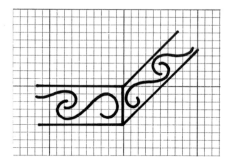

Starting to Work

Bind off the raw edges of your canvas with tape. I know it sounds silly, but don't forget to remove the tape when you are ready to make up the finished work.

There are two ways to work a pattern—from the border inward, and from the center outward. Designs with the major interest in the border are started from the outside, and conversely, designs with the major interest in the center are started in the center.

To work a border pattern such as the geese pillow on page 46 you must first make a few decisions. Will the patterned border be the outside edge of the pillow, or will there be an additional outside border of background color? Will the pillow be knife-edge or boxed? When these decisions are made you can measure, cut, and tape your canvas. Don't forget to leave at least two inches of canvas outside your outer dimensions—you will need this leeway when you stretch and finish the pillow. Also, it is an excellent place to try new stitches.

Now start your border pattern in the upper-right-hand corner of the canvas and the pattern. Work the entire border —COUNT CAREFULLY or you won't meet up correctly. If you are tempted to do a bit of the background as you work the border—RESIST THE TEMPTATION. Remember that if you make a mistake in the border and the background is filled in you will have to rip both the border and the background to correct your mistake in the border. It just isn't worth it! Finish the border—know that it is correct—then do the background. If you like to have two different kinds of work to do at the same time, work on two different canvases, not on two parts of one canvas.

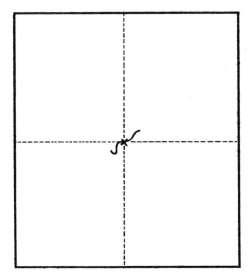

To work a center pattern locate the center of the canvas by folding the canvas as illustrated. Mark the center—either tie a piece of colored thread in the center or work around leaving the center stitches unworked. You will want to refer to this point often, so don't remove the marker until you have finished the rest of the canvas.

Now, locate the center of the design by folding it in the same way you folded the canvas. Start working out from the center. This way you will be able to feel the shape of the figure as it appears under your needle. Nothing is more exciting—it is what keeps me up into the late hours and drives my usually very patient husband absolutely WILD!

Working Canvas

I like to roll the ends of the canvas to keep it out of the way, to keep it from pulling out of shape, and to keep it clean. Four diaper pins are an easy way to hold the ends of the rolled canvas—or you may weave a thread through and then tie it. When you do the background you may want to roll all but the area you are working—it's much more manageable and your completed work will stay clean.

If you like to draw your designs on the canvas *please* make 100 per cent sure the marker you use is clearly marked *waterproof.* Many lovely, carefully worked designs have come to a disastrous end when they are dampened for stretching because the marker was not waterproof and the drawing bleeds through the needlework.

If you prefer to paint the pattern on the canvas, use oil or acrylic paints. Acrylic paint is water based so it is easier to work with and it is indelible once it dries. Thin the acrylic with water—you do not want thick paint as it will clog the mesh and make it difficult to work. When you paint, place your pattern under the canvas and trace it onto the canvas with the paint.

It's a good idea to keep a tube of white acrylic paint handy. Sometimes, as you work a design, you may want to change a line or relocate a flower or an initial. Just paint it out with the white paint. Sometimes a thread doesn't quite cover the outline on the canvas. Before you do the background, very carefully paint over the offending line.

Working Crewel

Most of the designs in this book are done in crewel and needlepoint on canvas, but many of them would be lovely in pure crewel. To illustrate, I have done the fish pillow on linen and on canvas (see pages 21, 23).

To change the scale of any of the designs, you may draw them first on ten-point graph paper and then transfer them to larger or smaller graph paper. The proportions will remain constant. If you are not sure of your drawing skill and don't want to use graph paper, you can have the design photostatted. Since the only thing you are interested in is the outline of the design you need only get the negative photostat—this will save you a little money.

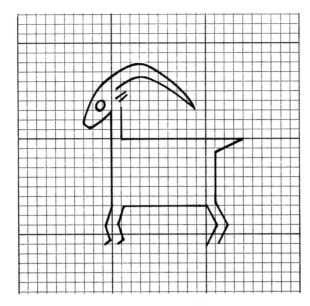

10-point graph paper

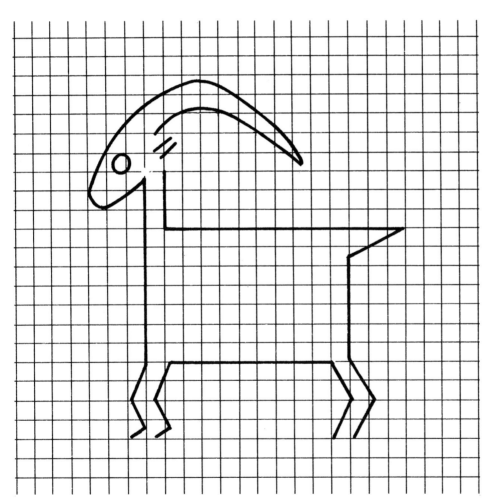

5-point graph paper

Now you have the design ready to transfer to fabric. This is best done with tracing paper and dressmakers carbon.

1 Select your piece of fabric and bind off the raw edges with tape. Leave two inches on all sides and don't forget to remove the tape when you are finished.

2 Trace the pattern onto tracing paper.

3 Spread the fabric flat on a hard surface. Stretch the fabric as square as possible. Iron it if necessary. If the fabric has a clear warp and woof use them as guidelines for the border and the corners.

Right

Wrong

Counting the threads is eye wearing, but the results are so professional that it's worth it! When you work with a fabric that doesn't show its warp and woof you must measure constantly to make sure the pattern doesn't grow or shrink.

4 Lash the fabric with tape so it will not wrinkle or move. Lay the dressmakers carbon on top of the fabric, and tracing paper pattern on top of the carbon. Clip or weight the fabric, carbon, and tracing paper sandwich so it doesn't shift as you work.

5 Using either a tracing wheel or a sharp pencil punch around the traced pattern. Press very hard to make sure the image is transferred.

6 When the pattern is punched, slowly undo one corner of the sandwich. Check to see if the design was transferred. If not, replace the sheets and re-punch. Remove the sheets. If you have a ghostly image you may *very carefully* and *very delicately* go over the punch marks with indelible laundry pen or a sharp 100 per cent waterproof marker. Use these sparingly as you don't want to see dark marks under the finished work.

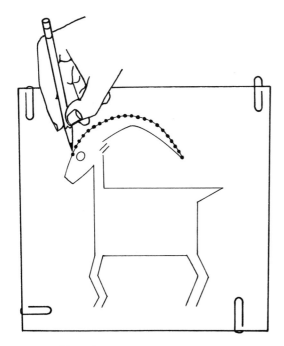

Punching the pattern

Needlepoint and Crewel Together

As already pointed out, these designs can be done in either crewel or needlepoint. I have worked them in both styles, but I prefer to work on canvas using a combination of the two. Combining the styles gives the needleworker enormous flexibility: geometric and curvilinear designs can be combined and greater textural variations can be created. For example, in the turtle on page 18 the round shape and rough texture of the legs contrasts with the angular shape but smoother texture of the shell.

In mixing stitches it is generally better to limit the variety of stitches used in each design. This prevents a superfluity of detail from overwhelming the design itself. An exception to this can be seen in the abstract table top on page 28. Here the design is so strong that the great variety of stitches does not weaken the total affect at all. A glossary of stitches used in the designs begins on page 73.

The colors used in each design are noted with each pattern. The numbers refer to the color chart of Paterna Persian Yarn.

12   One of the greatest thrills is to work over a simple design and make it your own. With this in mind I have included in each section a design for your experimentation and pleasure (see pages 13, 31, 39, 47, 69, 70). Improvise! Needlework is fun—enjoy it! !

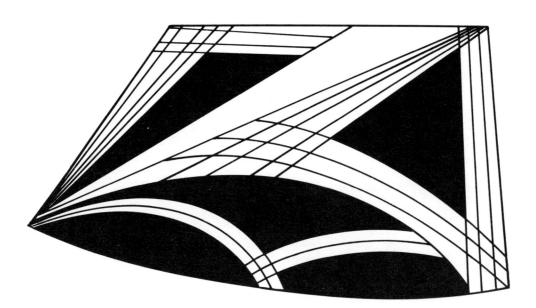

From the neck of a water jar, Old Zuni, New Mexico

Where

The patterns are chosen from works done in North America over a period of many centuries and in many geographic locations.

The tribes of North America can be grouped into regions sharing environmental, social, linguistic, and cultural similarities. Naturally, these regions do not have exact boundaries—peripheral tribes have characteristics of adjacent groups and groups sharing closer environmental ties. Of the many regions of the North American continent I have picked four from which to select the designs: the Southwest, the Great Plains, the Pacific Northwest, and the Eastern Woodlands.

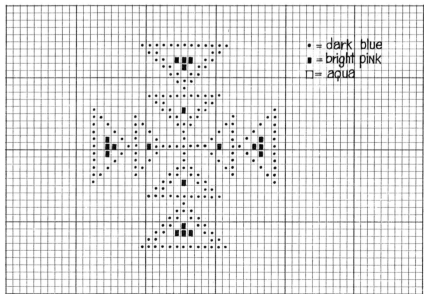

From a beaded belt, Jicarilla Apache, New Mexico

The Southwest

The peoples of the Mimbres Valley, near Tucson, Arizona, had a superb sense of design and good clay available. Good climate—not as dry as at present—and available food and water encouraged these peoples to settle and develop as village dwellers. They decorated their pottery with animal designs and abstract designs of great charm and sophistication. The Mimbres Valley culture vanished before the arrival of the white man. The turtle and the goat, the quail and the fish date from *c.* 1000 A.D. to 1300 A.D. The rust and white designs are earlier than the black and white designs and may date before 1000 A.D. The abstract bowl is from a neighboring area.

An interesting note: you will notice that many of the bowls have holes in the bottom. This is not a sign of age! These bowls were buried with their owners. Since the man was dead and could travel to the afterlife, the bowl too must be dead if it was to travel with its owner. Therefore, the bowls were "punched" or "killed" before burial.

The Turtle and the Goat

These two animals have been done as an unmatched pair of enormous cushions. They could, however, be made into marvelous rugs, or on ten-point canvas, into lovely pillows. The illustrations with each pattern show them flat and boxed. The border designs are included for finishing the designs either way.

A word of warning about five-point canvas and heavy wool. A single strand of heavy wool in a light color covers the canvas without trouble, but with dark wool the white canvas peeks through. Doubling the thread is too cumbersome and unnecessary as the canvas only peeks through. I painted the dark sections of the canvas with acrylic paint and then worked them. Acrylic paints come in a large variety of colors and are easy to use. The color need not match exactly so long as it is *darker* than the wool.

The Goat   5-point penelope canvas
4½″ deep
26 x 27½ top
Colors: green—507   tomato—260
This rather startled-looking fellow is drawn to scale with

the turtle which follows. The original border is particularly handsome in both the flat and boxed designs. Both patterns are included.

1 The body is done in stem stitch for texture and flexibility.

2 The eye is spider-web stitch—done very fat to make him a bit startled looking—and tacked down in the center to keep it from moving off center.

3 The background and the "Z" areas of the border are basketweave.

4 The "Z" itself is stem stitch.

5 The border around the top and around the base are cross stitch.

6 The vertical stripes on the border are stem stitch.

7 The border for the boxed pattern: The "Z" pattern is 33 stitches wide, the verticle stripes are 6 stitches wide—39 stitches for the whole design. This will make a continuous border.

8 The border for a flat design such as a rug or knife-edge pillow: Use the 33-stitch "Z" pattern and reapportion the number of vertical stem stitches to fill the length you wish. Fill in the transitional corner with the corner design.

The Goat

Possible corner for this border. If this is used, the "Z" pattern must abut the corner pattern on both sides. To achieve this, add more vertical stripes between the "Z" areas so the "Z" areas will be at both ends of the sides.

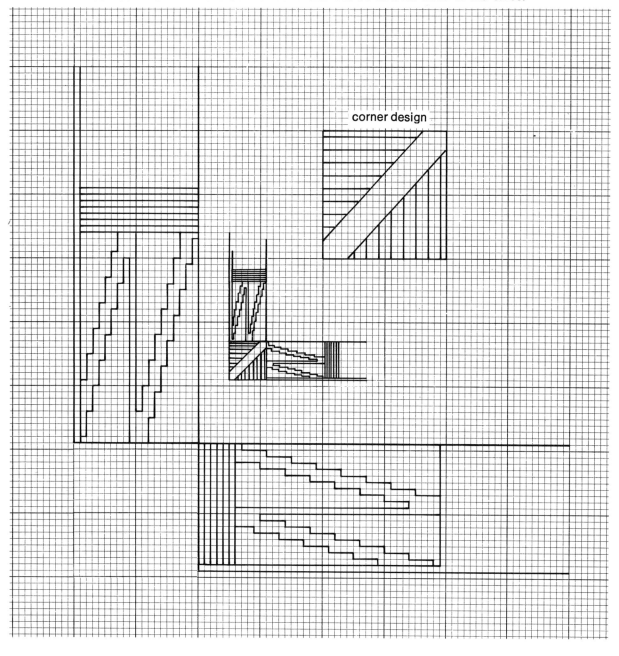

corner design

The Turtle 5-point penelope canvas
4½" deep
26 x 27½ top
Colors: rust—225 beige—496

1 The outline of each panel of the shell is cross stitch. This sets it off from the center of the shell and gives textural variety.

2 The center of each shell and the background are continental stitch—basketweave whenever possible, please!

3 The legs, outline of the head, and the eyes are stem stitch.

4 The neck and head are satin stitch anchored by a dark herringbone overlay.

5 Boxed border: The scroll in the border is stem stitch. The background is basketweave. Each side of the border is edged in a row of cross stitch. Reverse the pattern on each end to complete the border as illustrated on page 6.

6 Flat border: Use the same border as the boxed design, but omit the two rows of cross stitch at the corners and continue the scroll into the corner. Then use one of the suggested corner designs to fill out the square.

The Turtle

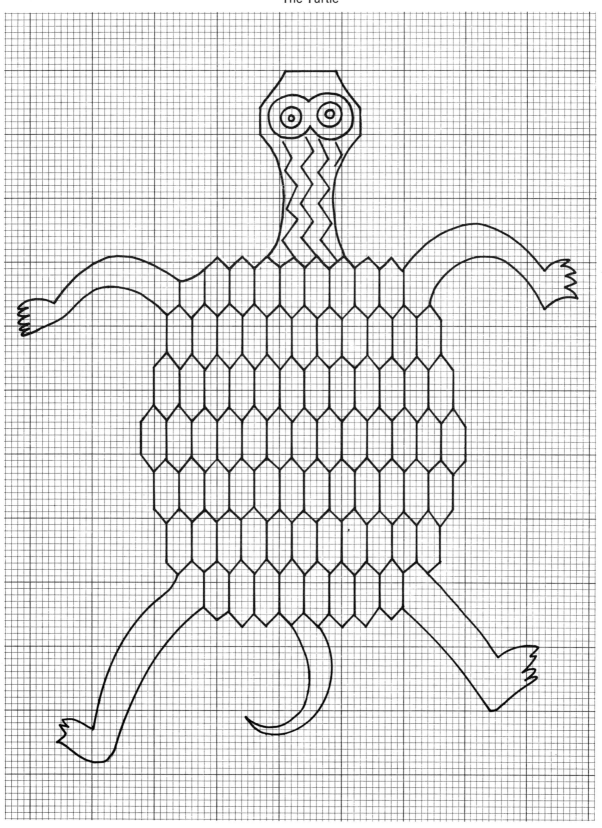

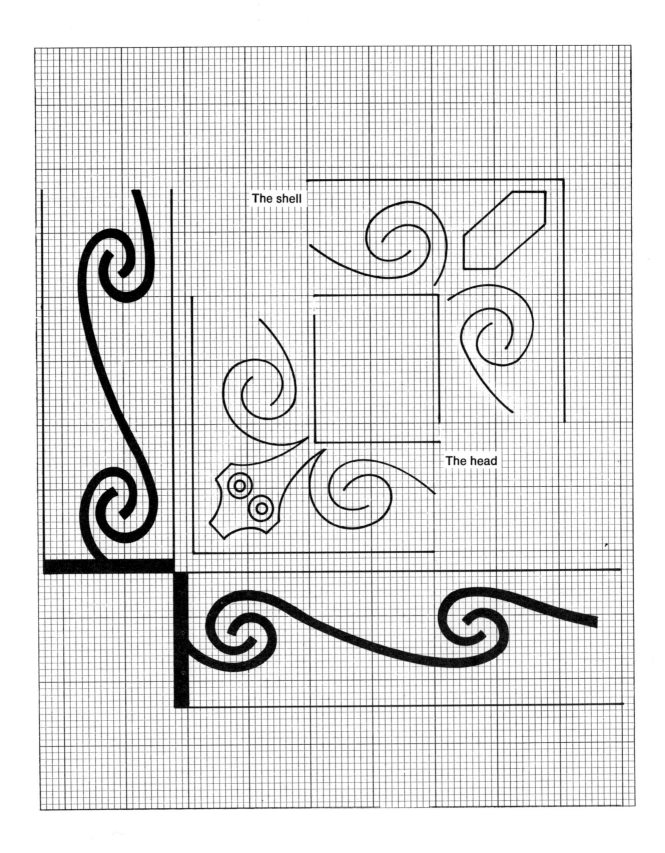

The shell

The head

Mimbres Valley Bowl and Goat Cushion

Mimbres Valley Bowl and Turtle Cushion

Mimbres Valley Bowl and Fish Pillows

Mimbres Valley Bowl and Quail Pillow

Southwest Bowl and Abstract Table Top

Arapaho Buckskin Vest and Camel Hair Vest

Omaha Beaded Vest and Needlework Stool

Omaha Beaded Belt and Floral Belt

Tlingit Basket and Whale and Gull Belt

Crewel Pillow

The Fish

The fish is done in crewel on linen and in crewel and needlepoint on canvas to show you how easily these designs can be adapted to your favorite kind of needlework.

Crewel Pillow   The crewel pillow is done on coarse natural linen.

1   The head and scales are split stitch.
2   The gills, fin, and tail are chain stitch.
3   The five "feet" are buttonhole stitch.
4   The blue scales are tied laid work.

The border: The original border was a simple three-row design, reading from the outside inward—

(1) 3 rows chain stitch, then a space;
(2) 1 row stem stitch, then a space;
(3) 2 rows chain stitch.

I wanted something more elaborate. To keep the border in tune with the fish I used fish-oriented stitches, reading from the outside inward—

(1) fly stitch, fishbone shaped;
(2) seed stitch;
(3) stem stitch;
(4) 2 rows of chain stitch;
(5) single feather stitch to look like a fish hook, with a seed stitch inside as "bait."

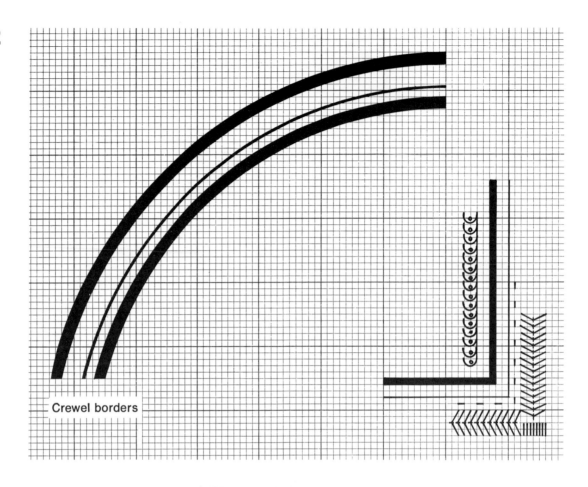

Crewel borders

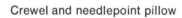

Crewel and needlepoint pillow

10-point penelope canvas

2″ deep

13 x 13 top

Colors: dark brown—112   dark blue—385   light blue—
    743   beige—513

2 strands of wool except when noted

This pillow is a mate to the quail which is the next design.

1   Outline the fish in stem stitch.

2   The eye is spider web stitch.

3   The gills are stem stitch.

4   The head, fin, and tail are rice stitch.

5   For the scales, lay out a three-layer grid, covering each design line with wool.

Then at each three-way intersection, tack the threads down —like tied laid work—with a single thread.

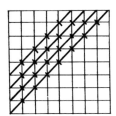

6   Fill the brown scales and the dark blue scales with satin stitch.

7   The pale blue scales are continental stitch with the tied laid work in a single strand of brown.

The border, reading from the outside inward is:

(1)   2 rows of rice stitch in brown;

(2)   2 rows of stem stitch in dark blue;

(3)   7 rows of continental stitch in dark blue overlaid with single-strand tied laid work in pale blue;

(4)   2 rows of stem stitch in dark blue;

(5)   1 row of rice stitch in brown.

The background is encroaching gobelin stitch.

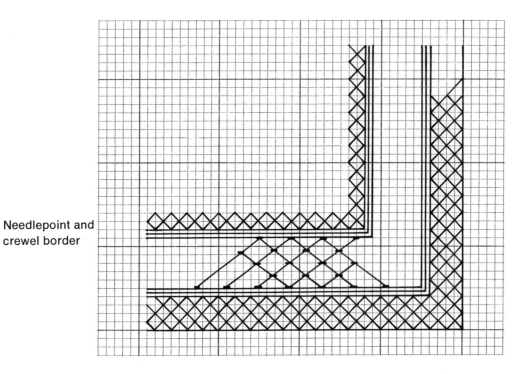

Needlepoint and
crewel border

The Fish

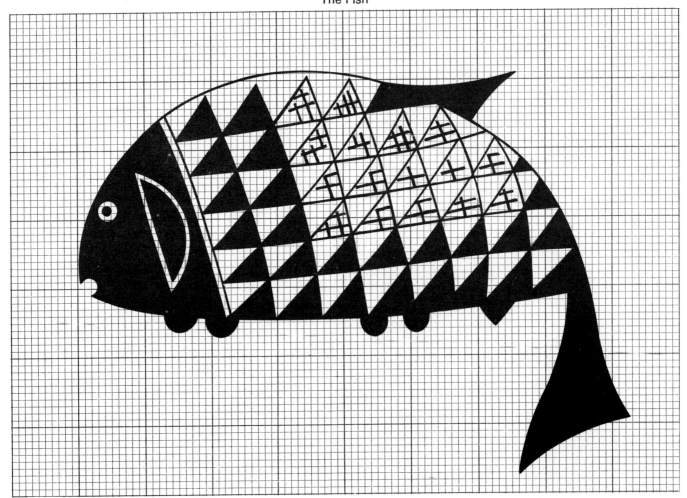

The Quail

10-point penelope canvas
2″ deep
13 x 13 top
Colors: the same as the fish in the preceding pattern.
2 strands of wool except when noted
The quail is finished as a mate to the needlepoint fish.
1 Outline the bird in stem stitch.
2 Put in the areas of stem stitch: (a) on either side of the cross-hatched pattern on the body; (b) on the two right-angle areas on the wing; (c) at the end of the tail.
3 Make a large pop-eyed spider web stitch eye. This must be exaggerated to give his surprised look.
4 Fill in the tip of the tail, the body, and wing sections with rice stitch.
5 Satin stitch the feathers, alternating lighter and darker shades of blue.
6 Satin stitch the legs.
7 Fill in the remaining tail section, wing section, and tummy with continental stitch in the darker blue using three strands of wool.

8 On the tail and wing do tied laid work using a single thread of lighter blue between every two rows—one series vertical and one series horizontal. Tack the threads at each intersection—always tacking in the same direction.

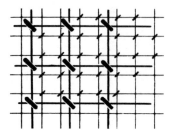

9 The tummy is overlaid and tacked the same way, but done twice. First, in brown every two rows, vertically and horizontally and tacked diagonally. Second, in light blue on the diagonal so as to bisect every other row of the lower brown squares. The blues are tacked horizontally. (As a crewel stitch this is called trellis filling.)

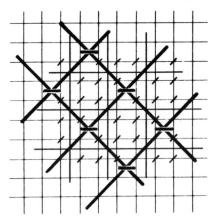

10 The border and the background are the same as the fish (see page 23 for instructions).

An alternate border is shown. This is a particularly good border if the quail is done in crewel on linen. It is a repeat of the feather design:

(1) 2 rows of rice stitch;

(2) 7 rows of feather design, executed with stem stitch and satin stitch filling in alternating colors just like the tail and wing of the quail;

(3) 1 row of brown stem stitch;

(4) 2 rows of beige stem stitch;

(5) 1 row of brown rice stitch.

The Quail and alternate border design

Abstract Table Top

10-point penelope canvas
13½ " in diameter
Colors: dark—R 80   light—454
2 strands of wool except when noted

This bowl fascinates me. It bugs me too! It was the first design I attempted and the results were disastrous! But I couldn't discard the design. It is too strong and too timeless. It is one of the oldest pieces in this book, yet how completely twentieth century it is!

Exactly twelve months after the first disastrous attempt, I tried again. The result seems more satisfactory and it was fun to do, so maybe that's a good time to stop. However, you may have a better answer. Give it a try!

You will notice that the design, although it appears to be symmetrical, is really very irregular. That is not just me! The original artist painted freehand inside the bowl with a soft brush. The design is reversed, but not mirrored. I am convinced that the small irregularities keep the design from becoming a mechanical exercise—preserving a feeling of movement and vitality. Of course, for the needleworker this is a boon—we don't have to count every stitch! The similar areas are done in the same color and stitch, but the areas vary slightly in size and shape.

When you lay your canvas on top of the design to trace it you will make the stitching job much easier if you place the straight lines of the R-shaped areas directly on top of the vertical threads in the canvas.

With this design the easiest way to designate areas is with numbers on the drawing so each area can be discussed without confusing it with similarly shaped areas.

Start by outlining the entire design in stem stitch.

1 Work a brick stitch through all the vertical threads, skipping every other horizontal thread. This gives a smaller, smoother stitch than the usual brick stitch which uses every other vertical penelope space.

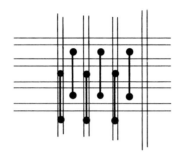

2 Continental stitch using three strands of wool.

3 Superimpose on the continental stitch a bump stitch based on five stitches by five stitches.

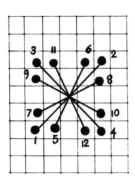

Make sure you do all the bumps the same way so the tops look alike. These bumps may be scattered more irregularly than shown, if you wish.

4 Satin stitch, alternating colors.

5 Continental stitch using three strands of wool.

6 Satin stitch.

7 Alternate rows of satin stitch using all vertical threads for one color and all horizontal threads for the other color. You will notice that the beginning and end of each stitch shares the hole with the stitch going perpendicular to it. You will get a herringbone effect as shown here.

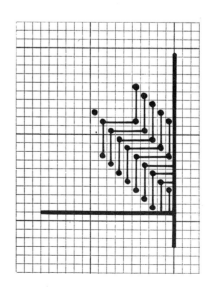

Abstract Table Top

8 Satin stitch four rows.

9 Continental stitch.

10 Rice stitch.

11 Stem stitch, alternating one row of the darker color with two rows of the lighter color.

12 Half cross stitch and continental stitch, alternating colors and direction.

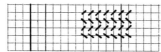

13 Stem stitch, alternating colors.

14 Upright cross stitch.

15 Encroaching gobelin stitch.

This is *your* design from the Mimbres Valley to do as you wish—in crewel, in needlepoint, or in a combination. The animals appear as drawn, feet to feet, but they can be used any way you like. Have fun!

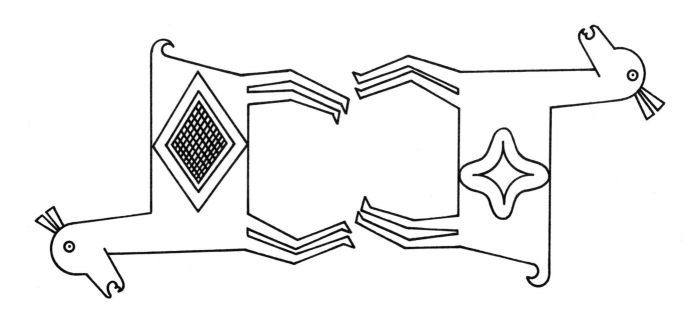

From a Mimbres Valley bowl

The Great Plains

These peoples were big-game hunters, dependent on buffalo and deer for food, clothing, tools, and artifacts. Before the Spaniards introduced horses to North America the Plains Indians used dogs as their beasts of burden, so their wanderings were relatively confined. With the availability of horses in the eighteenth century, the Plains Indians began traveling longer and longer distances in search of the dwindling herds.

We know these tribes only after the white man started to travel across their country. Unfortunately, the same white man who found these people also caused the weakening of the Indian cultures through the transmission of disease, territorial restrictions, wars, and extracultural influences such as guns and alcohol.

Early decoration was limited to painting on hides, usually stories of great hunts or religious ceremonies. With the acquisition of the iron needle, the Indian women increasingly began to embroider with porcupine quills and shell beads dyed in bright colors. These decorations were lively and uninhibited. Much later European traders brought bright glass beads to trade with the Indians. The embroiderers went WILD—all the traditional designs were even more beautiful in glass beads. Even later the designs were influenced by European forms.

Porcupine embroidery and beadwork make lovely needlework designs. The designs here are late—some are of this century—but their quality is in no way affected by their vintage.

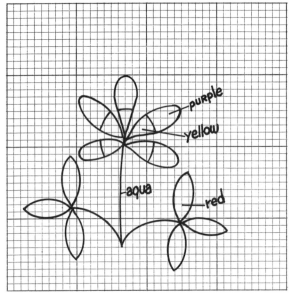

Porcupine embroidery from an Arapaho buckskin vest

Camel Hair Vest

Colors: black and white   red—843   aqua—755   orange
—970   pink—659

This marvelously alive and entertaining vest is a page from
a history book: flags, feathers, Indian ponies—it's all right
there! Our hero, covered in glory, is immortalized on the vest
by an Arapaho squaw who tells the story on buckskin with
porcupine quill embroidery. The design is simplicity itself.
There are only three stitches used: split stitch for all the
stems and flag poles, buttonhole stitch for the lapel, and
satin stitch for everything else.

The vest is done in crewel on camel hair, but there is no
reason why the same stitches couldn't be done on canvas
with a smooth stitch like the brick stitch or the encroaching
gobelin for the background.

A word of warning. The brave this belonged to was *tiny,*
so the proportions are a bit out of whack. Before you start
this vest get your tailor to give you a paper pattern for a vest
that will fit. Then space the design on that pattern.

Some of the design elements have been omitted because I
felt it was a bit cluttered. However, the entire design is repro-
duced so you may judge for yourself.

Vest, front

Vest, back

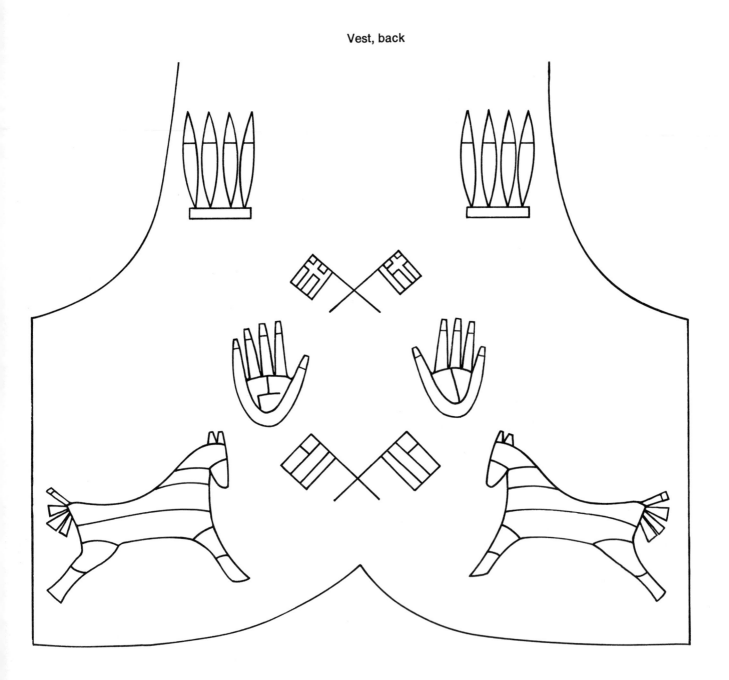

Floral Belt and Stool

These lovely pieces of beadwork were purchased for The Museum of Natural History in 1930 by Dr. Margaret Mead from the Omaha Indians in Macy, Nebraska. The style and treatment are similar.

The designs are equally suited to crewel on fabric, needle-point, or a combination of both on canvas. On canvas basket-weave, brick stitch or a gobelin stitch could be used for the background.

By rearranging the elements of designs you can adapt these designs for such things as suitcase racks, pillows, rugs, chair seats, or book covers.

The belt: The pattern of the belt can be lengthened by removing the curled leaf at the end of the belt and inserting any number of flower and grape repeats. Replace the curled leaf to finish the pattern.

The vest: The front panel design can be divided into three sections (marked ———→). You may lengthen this design to your needs by repeating any sections of the design or by stretching the stem at these points. The back panel can be adapted in the same way. Do not, however, stretch the stems too far as much of the strength of the design is dependent on the tension created by compactness in the design.

Floral Belt

12-point penelope canvas
25″ long
Colors: black and white   purple—640   green—G 74
  orange—444   aqua—748   yellow—F 56
2 strands of wool except when noted

1   Stem stitch the vine in black.

2   Outline the flowers and leaves in stem stitch.

3   Fill in the flowers and leaves with satin stitch, using the direction of the canvas to guide the stitches.

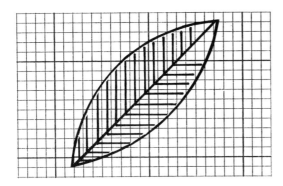

4   Overlay the veins in the leaves with a single strand of black.

5   The grapes are overstuffed spider stitch tacked in the center to keep them from moving.

6   The background is straight gobelin stitching between each vertical penelope thread.

7   The border is also straight gobelin, but it is mitered at the corners to make a frame.

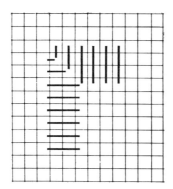

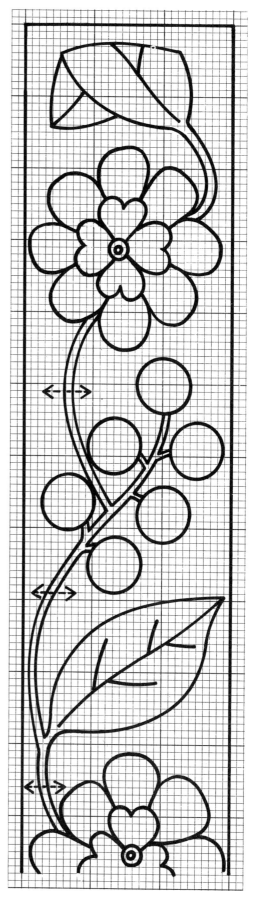

Floral belt

Floral Stool

10-point penelope canvas
21 x 17 inches
Colors: black and white   dark green—520   light green—
    555   blue—323   aqua—322   yellow—450   rust—245
2 strands of wool except when noted

Only the back of the vest has been used in making the stool and it has been stretched as described above to fill the size of the stool cushion. The design of the front panels is included for your enjoyment. The patterns are drawn like the vest—unstretched.

The vine is stem stitch. It may be done in black or dark blue. The rust flowers and the blue leaves are satin stitch. The yellow and green flowers are stem stitch. You may prefer, however, to make all the flowers and leaves stem stitch.

The background is brick stitch as described in step 1 on page 29.

Finally each flower is outlined in a single thread in the stem stitch. Thus the pattern and the background will meet perfectly—no gaps and no crushed filling stitches.

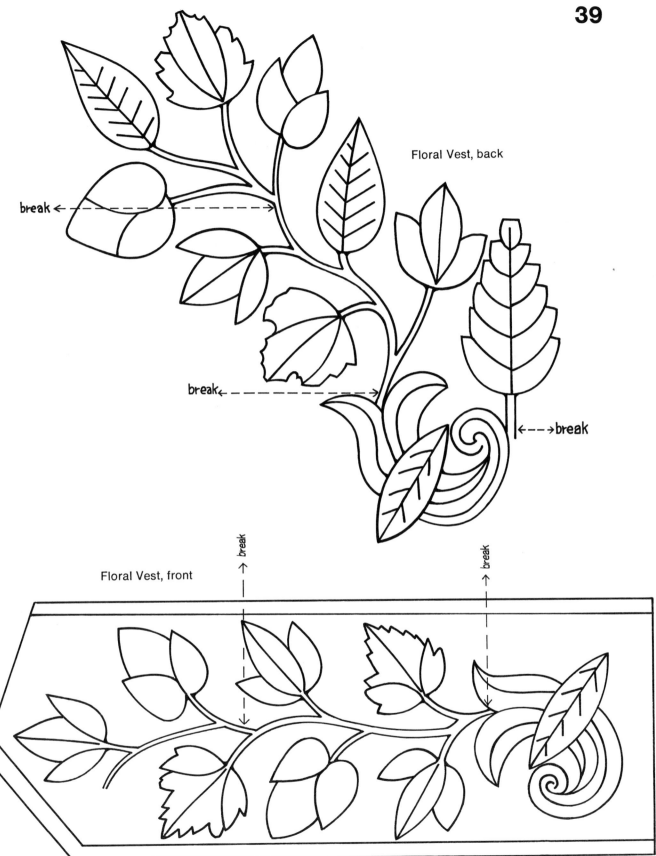

break

break

break

Floral Vest, back

Floral Vest, front

break

break

The Pacific Northwest

The tribes living along the northwest coast of the United States and Canada are quite unique. These people do not follow the general rules of cultural development from gatherer to farmer to semi-leisured inventive man. These peoples remained gatherers as there was never any need to turn to agriculture to sustain life. A superabundance of fish, fowl, and berries gave these peoples leisure time to develop their cultures early in their development. Salmon ran seasonally, wild birds flew seasonally, and berries grew seasonally. Once these peoples discovered ways of preserving their food supplies they could move into a rhythmical pattern of existence, alternating between hunting and preserving on the one hand, and complete leisure on the other.

In addition to this freedom for cultural development these peoples were blessed with limitless supplies of materials with which to develop their crafts. The Japanese current which runs along the Pacific coastline keeps the climate mild and moist all year round. Enormous forests and lush grasses abound. The cedar trees are magnificent, providing wood for carving and boat building, and bark for clothing and yarn making.

We identify these peoples mostly with their stupendous totem poles. Children gawk and adults wonder at these tall statues peopled by strange and wonderful creatures.

I have chosen, however, to use designs from the baskets woven by the Tlingit people. They are equally inventive and appealing—and they are newer to our eyes.

The baskets made by the Tlingit are a marvel. They were used to hold water, and to cook in—facts that are hard to believe until you see this remarkable weaving. The weaving is incredibly tight and the pattern completely geometrical. To increase the size of the basket at the top, the weaver has gradually increased the spacing of the weft—no added warp, no expanded design—all done in the process of the weaving

The Tlingit use "yarn" made of cedar bark for both the warp and the weft. The decoration is woven into the basket by a process called imbrication. As the weaver works the warp and the weft, grasses of different natural colors or dyed with natural dyes are wrapped around the weft, superimposing a design that becomes part of the basket. The designs are geometrical or animal. The geometric are wonderfully bold and the animals are direct and humorous.

With these designs I have sometimes combined patterns from different baskets. You may prefer to use them separately or in different combinations. Experiment—have a good time!

Whale and Gull Belt

12-point penelope canvas
25" long
Colors: pale pink—837 dark purple—610 purple—612
  dark mauve—615 medium mauve—618 mauve—620
2 strands of wool except when noted

This fat, pleasant-looking whale doesn't look much like a killer whale. Perhaps he has already feasted and is content. He doesn't seem to be at all interested in his fellow ocean-dweller, the gull. The basket weaver was not trying to tell us anything about the habits of these animals or their relationship to each other. They are decorative elements only. A wonderfully amusing, happy pair.

This pattern can be made shorter or longer by either placing the animals closer together or further apart. Decide on your length and then lay out the pattern and decorative fillers to fill your space.

Each animal was first outlined in stem stitch with a single thread in the area color. Each "flagpole" was stem stitched in a single thread. All the other areas are basketweave.

All the whales are the dark purple, but all the other areas are varied from repeat to repeat to avoid a feeling of mechanical repetition.

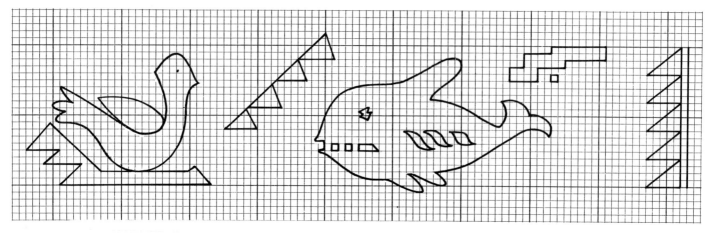

Whale and Gull Belt

Celadon Pillow

10-point mono canvas
18 x 18 inches square
Colors: dull brown—124   apricot—467   orange—444
    yellow—458   celadon—593
3 strands of wool except when noted

This pillow is a composite of two Tlingit basket designs. You may vary the size and shape in a number of ways: by changing or eliminating the outside background border, or by reducing or increasing or rearranging the number of repeats in the decorative border.

End patterns finish design

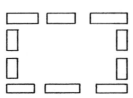

End patterns enclosed, top and bottom

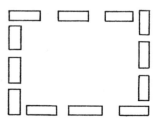

Pattern turns at each corner

The entire pillow is done in the continental and basket-weave stitches.

The overlay goes from hole to hole covering three vertical threads with each overstitch. The overlay is done with two strands of wool in either a lighter shade than the background or with wool from a different dye lot than the background—the shading should be very slight.

Do the decorative border first, then fill in the background, and finally do the overlay.

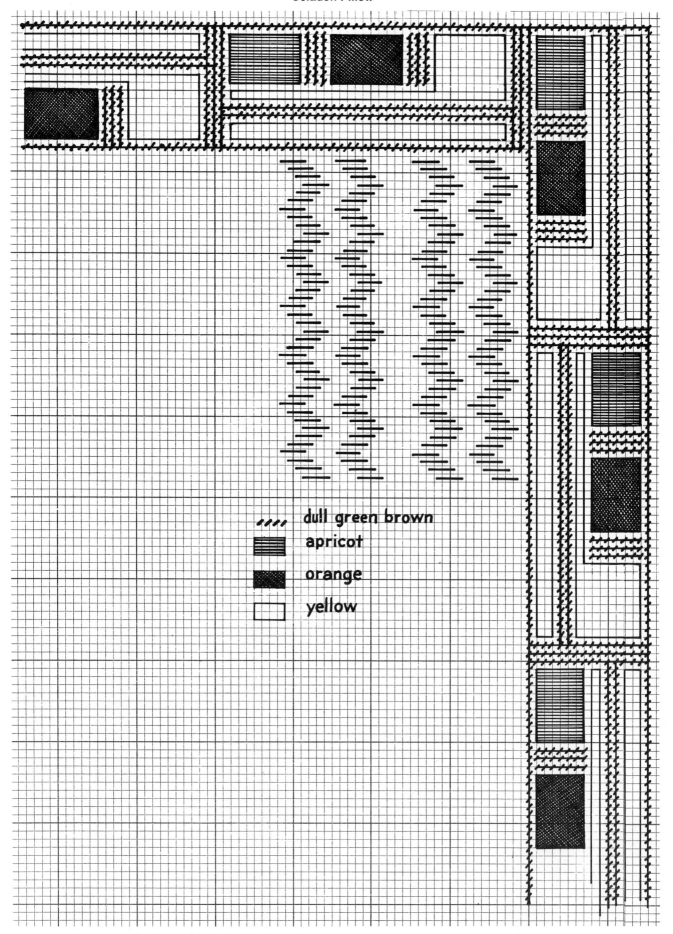

dull green brown
apricot
orange
yellow

Orange and Pink Pillow

10-point mono canvas
10 x 10 inches
Colors: orange—978   pink—659
3 strands of wool

The orange and pink pillow is a variation of the center overlay pattern of the preceding pillow—a more contemporary version.

Each triangle of the pillow is treated the same, but the direction of the stitches in each triangle runs perpendicular to those in the other triangle. This is accomplished by com-

46

pleting one triangle and then giving the canvas a quarter turn and completing the second triangle.

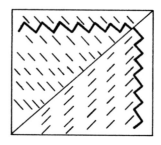

You will note a slight variation in the overlay pattern.

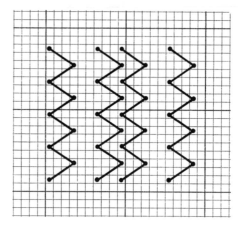

This overlay is done with only a single strand of wool. If you wish a fuller effect use two strands as in the preceding pillow.

The center diagonal is accented with a single row of uncut turkey stitch done with a three-strand thread of mixed colors. The tassels are also mixed colors.

To make mixed strands, separate the three strands of each color and remix them one by one. Mixing the strands one at a time gives a softer, puffier look to the final effect.

Geese Pillow

10-point penelope canvas
14 x 14 inches
Colors: dark brown—140   medium brown—462   beige—
492   yellow—437
3 strands of wool except when noted

This boxed pillow is also a composite of two Tlingit baskets. All the work is done in the basket stitch except the outline of the geese which is stem stitch in one strand of wool.

Start this pattern in the upper-right-hand corner working around the border. When the border is complete, trace the bird patterns—each one once and one twice—so you will have five different tracings. Cut roughly around each tracing and then arrange them around the center area until you are happy with the arrangement. Draw them on the canvas. Outline each bird with a single strand of the color which matches the adjacent body area—yellow on the beak, medium brown on the body, etc. Fill in the bodies of the geese and, finally, fill in the background.

Note that the extra rows added for turn-under are an extension of the outside row, so that if the sewing machine slips slightly when the welting is stitched on, the pattern will be the same and the slip won't show.

The Geese

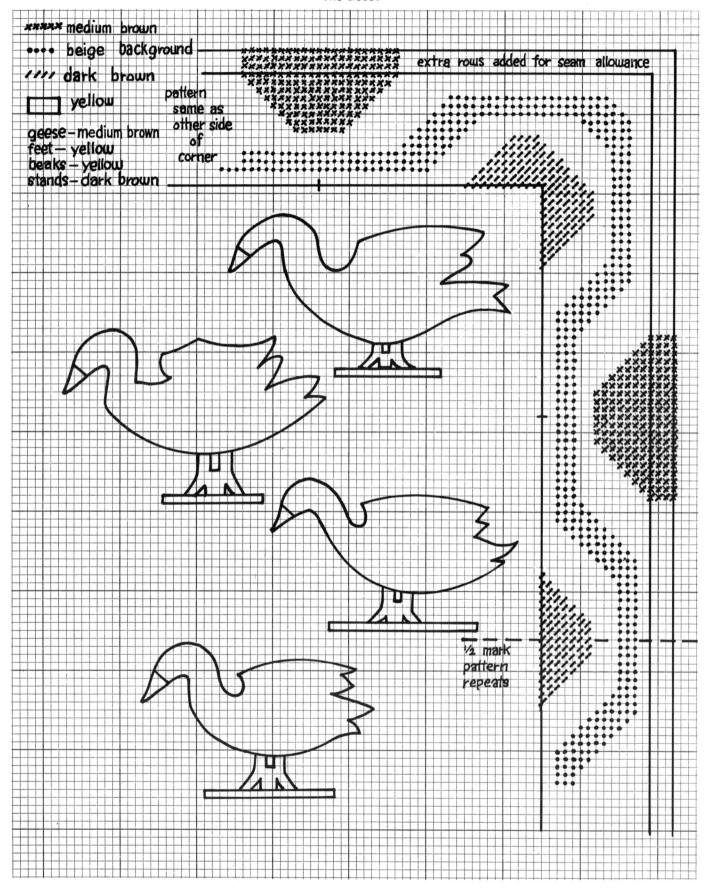

Here is a really angry killer whale and border for you to enjoy on your own.

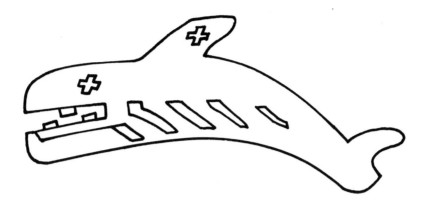

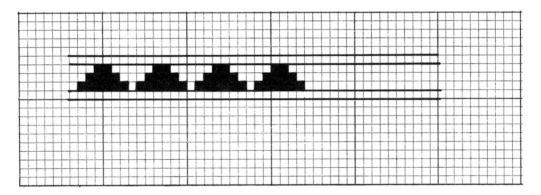

Killer Whale and border from a Tlingit basket

The Eastern Woodlands

This group, which covers the Northeast United States and Canada all the way to the Plains states, is not as cohesive as the other groups already discussed. The land area included in the grouping makes it easy to understand the variety, for it is natural that variations exist in an area this large.

The peripheral tribes often resemble their neighbors from different groups more than they resemble their own group. Some of the beadwork and porcupine quill embroidery done by the Woodland Indians closely resembles that done by the Plains Indians. I have tried to choose patterns that are not similar to give larger variety to this book, but you must understand that the lines of demarkation between groups are not always as clear as they seem here.

The Eastern Woodland Indians were mainly agricultural. Their favorite decorative element was floral—sometimes naturalistic and sometimes highly abstract. They thought that plants had "powers" and, thus, floral shapes became symbols of the plant "powers." The floral designs could therefore impart partial protection and power to the wearer or owner.

Porcupine embroidery antedates shell and bead embroidery. The Plains Indians used porcupine decoration primarily on buckskin while the Eastern Woodland Indians used it on buckskin and on birchbark. The rigidity of the quills does not inhibit the creativity of the Indian artists—how humorous and noble the Plains buckskin best is—and how sophisticated the Micmac boxes!

The Eastern Woodland Indians wove beautiful bags and fabrics. They used two methods of weaving, the compact weft and the spaced weft. These techniques are discussed with the needlepoint pieces.

Diagonal Pillow

10-point mono canvas
10 x 19 inches
Colors: blue—754   yellow—452   green—469
3 strands of wool except when noted

This design is taken from a basket woven by the Chitimacha Indians from the Mississippi Delta. Each layer of diagonals runs opposite to the diagonal beneath it, jarring the eye with color and design and creating a feeling of tension and excitement. If you wish to change the colors make sure that the colors you choose are of equal vibrancy or the full effect of the design will be weakened.

Count carefully. When I started to lay out the green overlay I went almost mad! Work slowly and refer to the drawing and the enlarged photograph constantly.

1 Decide how large you want your design to be, and measure your canvas so it is long enough. Then do the underneath diagonals in the basketweave stitch.

2 Start the overlay with two strands of wool in the upper-right-corner of the outside border and work until you have completed three sides.

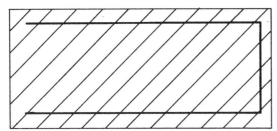

3 Now start the next inner band, and finally the third inner band—always leaving the fourth end open.

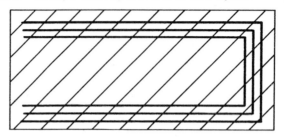

4 Start the center pattern at the right end, working the pattern again and again until you have reached the desired length.

5 Repeat the starting pattern in reverse.

Start

Finish

6 Then close in the three borders. By waiting until now you will be able to compensate for any misleading or miscounting along the way.

7 On the overlay the needle goes in between the already completed background stitches. Look carefully at the pattern and at this enlargement to avoid confusion on the corners.

8 The center overlay is tacked down every other strand with a two-strand thread of the same color as the background at that point.

(See complete diagram on page 53.)

Tlingit Baskets and Geese Pillow

Tlingit Baskets and Celadon Pillow

Tlingit Basket and Orange and Pink Pillow

Chitimacha Basket and Diagonal Pillow

Micmac Box Top and Celadon and White Stool

Micmac Box and Flame Box Top

Fox Bag and Checked Slipper

Fox Bag and Slipper

Winnebago Bag and Bargello Bag

Winnebago Needlecase and Velvet Needlecase

Malecite Cuff and Velvet Eyeglass Case

(See page 52.)

Celadon and White Stool

10-point penelope canvas
11 x 10½ inches not including the outer border
Colors: oyster—017   yellow—580   dark celadon—555
  celadon—570   light celadon—575
2 strands of wool except when noted

This stool is taken from the curved top of a birchbark box decorated with porcupine quills by the Micmac Indians of Nova Scotia. To work quills on skins, such as the buckskin vest on page 33, the quills were soaked in water and then flattened. On birchbark the quills were left round. The pattern was pricked into the skin or the bark and the two ends of the quills inserted and bent over. Finally the back of the piece was lined to keep the quills in place.

You will have to be willing to count this, but it is very rewarding. I think this piece gave me the greatest thrill of all as it took shape under my needle.

1 Find the center of the canvas and begin the pattern with the continental stitches around the two diamonds. The continental stitch changes direction at each corner so it looks like a running stitch. At each corner where the direction changes, the stitch is a cross stitch.

2 Do the satin stitching of the rectangular shapes next to the diamonds. *Each satin stitch must be straight.* Penelope canvas is very helpful here. Always put the needle up through and then down through the same vertical threads. On all the satin stitching *the thread goes between every vertical thread.* For a uniform puffed effect, keep the threads flat. Do not allow them to twist.

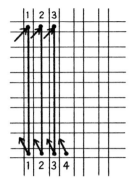

3 Do the satin stitching of the circles. The drawing is on ten-point graph paper in double scale to give you the right thread count for the ten-point penelope canvas which has twenty threads to the inch.

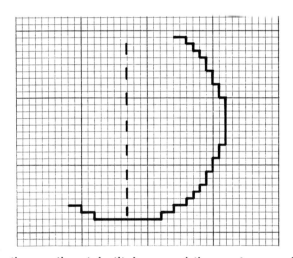

4 Do the continental stitch around the center panel.

5 Satin stitch the half moon shapes—again the graph is double scale, as above.

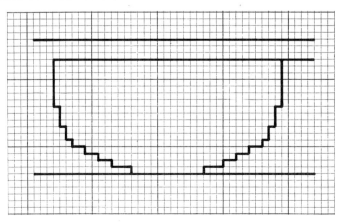

6 Satin stitch the larger rectangles.

7 Fill in the background areas with satin stitch.

8 Continental stitch around the half moon areas and into the corners of the border.

9 Satin stitch these areas of the border.

10 Fill in the border background.

11 Do the overlay accents. All of these are superimposed on other stitches and are done with a single strand of wool.

12 Continental stitch three rows around the border.

13 Outer border: this border will allow you to vary the size of the cushion to your needs—just vary the depth of the stitches. This stool has a 10-square-deep satin stitch outer border. The border may be boxed or knife edge. The boxed corner omits the corner and the knife edge decreases the length of the stitches in the corner to make a neat diagonal seam at the corner.

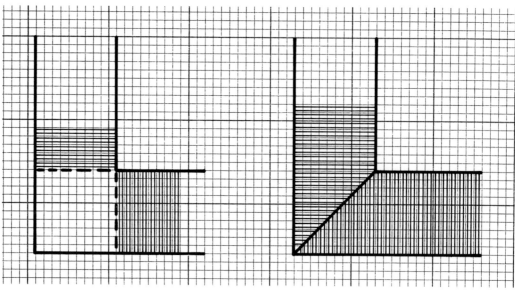

Boxed edge   Knife edge

Celadon Pillow

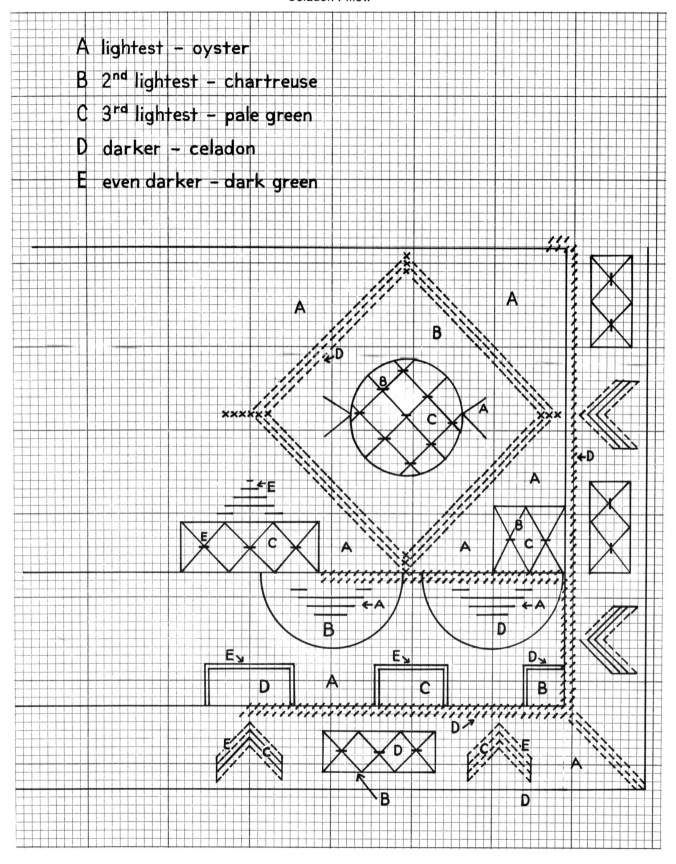

A lightest – oyster
B 2nd lightest – chartreuse
C 3rd lightest – pale green
D darker – celadon
E even darker – dark green

Flame Box Top

10-point penelope canvas

10½ x 3¾ inches

Colors: green—566   dark—958   medium—978
  pale—988   oyster—017

2 threads throughout

Like the stool in the preceding design, this lovely design is taken from a birchbark box decorated with porcupine quills by the Micmac Indians of Nova Scotia. In this case the design is from the end panel of the box. A marvelously effective design—and it is remarkably easy too! In addition, it is enormously flexible—you may increase the length or shorten the pattern by adding or omitting units; you may increase or decrease the width by adding or subtracting rows of the pattern, or by increasing or decreasing the outside border.

Any colors may be used, but I think it is most effective when three shades of one color, a related color, and a neutral color are used.

1   The secret of this design is the green (related color) square.

(a) The center of the square is between two narrow penelope threads—vertical and horizontal.

(b) Count out the square as shown. Then string square next to square until you have reached the length of your pattern.

(c) Fill in the center with neutral color. This is a two-part process. First, fill in the square with long satin stitches from upper right to lower left. Second, overlay four long satin stitches going from upper left to lower right.

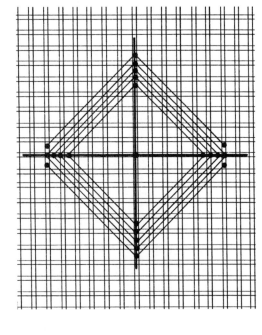

2 Now, like bargello, you follow the pattern established by the squares, always stitching between each penelope thread:

   (a) 4 rows of the pale shade;

   (b) 4 rows of the medium shade;

   (c) 4 rows of mixed strands made up of the dark and the medium shades;

   (d) 4 rows of the medium shade.

3 Fill in between with horizontal satin stitch in the neutral color.

4 Finish to the size you prefer using the border illustrated on page 53 in the neutral color.

Flame Box Top

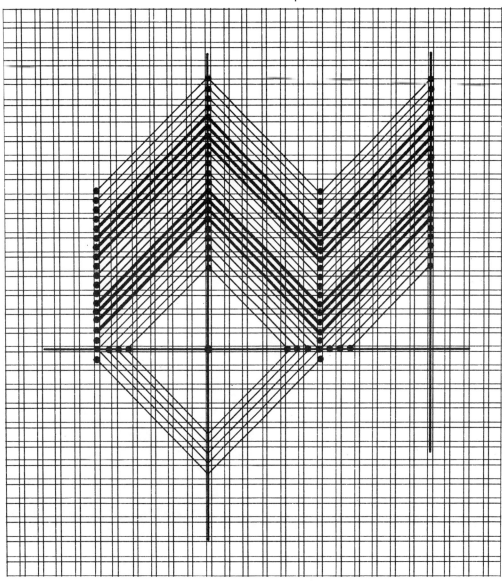

Slippers

10-point penelope canvas
Colors: pale blue—386   maroon—810   yellow—Y 68
    green—528   beige—015   dark blue—323
Threads noted on the pattern

10-point penelope canvas
Colors: yellow—Y 52   green—559   blue—742
Threads noted on the pattern

The two slipper patterns are based on a bag woven in the spaced weft method by the Fox Indians in Iowa. The space weft method of weaving is one of the most ancient in the world. There are Peruvian examples dating from 2000 B.C. As the name implies, the weft is spaced or separated and the pattern is created by moving the warp, or vertical, threads. Many attempts to imitate this weaving produced only one combination of stitches which was quite good, but it was much too bulky. So, I decided to find a combination of stitches to give the illusion of a spaced weft with the underneath color showing through.

Before getting into the details of this design let me say a word about the animals on the slippers. The Woodland Indians preferred floral motifs for decoration, but their gods were animals. The bird—or thunderbird—is the chief figure of the Upper world. The panther, on the other hand, is one of the Under world gods. The thunderbird and the panther are adversaries in myths of many of the Eastern Woodland tribes.

The thunderbird on a bag is a form of prayer for protection. The panther on a moccasin is a symbol of the fierceness and strength of the warrior who wears it. It seems fitting that the animals should be stitched on men's slippers: the Upper world thunderbird on the right and the Under world panther on the left.

There are two and sometimes three steps in creating the illusion of space weft weaving in needlepoint.

1   A tramé thread is layed down over the narrow pair of penelope threads. Note carefully the entrance and exit points of the tramé threads. (See page 62.)

Single-color tramé   Two-color tramé   Lazy stitch covering tramé

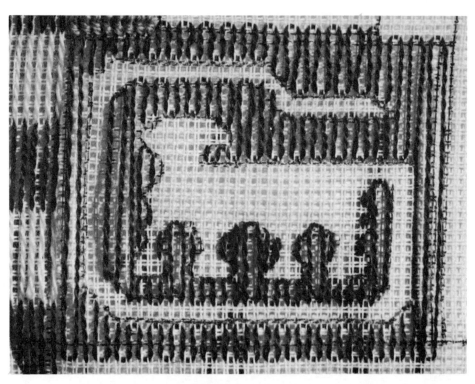

Animal pattern with one-color tramé stitched in, ready for second color to fill in the animal form

2 The tramé threads are stitched down with a lazy knit stitch—that is, a row of continental stitches followed by a row of half cross stitches.

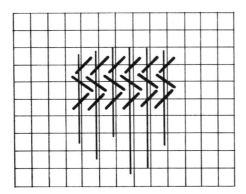

The openness of this stitch permits a bit of the tramé to show through—an illusion of the woven threads.

3 On the yellow, green, and blue slipper there is a third step—a backstitch of green between every other row of the lazy stitch.

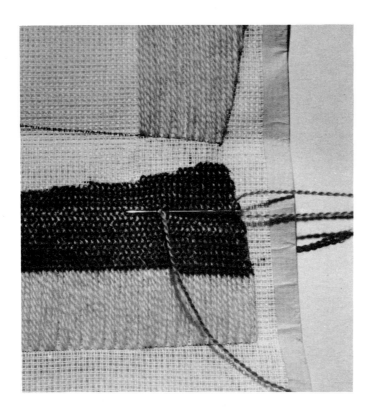

This is an imitation of the spaced weft. This step is omitted in the checked slippers as it seemed to be too busy, but you may want to add it if you use the pattern for a bag or a pillow.

Sometimes I have used a single-strand tramé with two-strand lazy stitch and sometimes the reverse. The specific instructions are on each pattern.

You will note that one pattern is for the left foot and the other for the right foot. The shape is slightly different for each foot, so be sure when you draw the patterns not to make two left feet by mistake!

Thunderbird

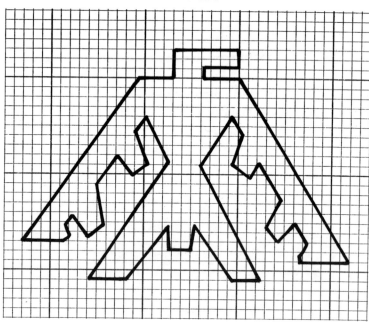

Underground Panther

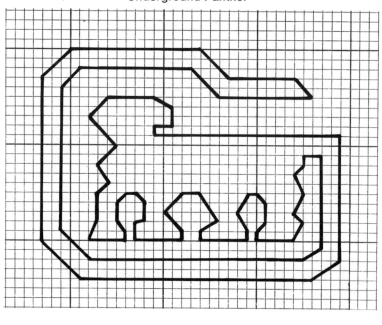

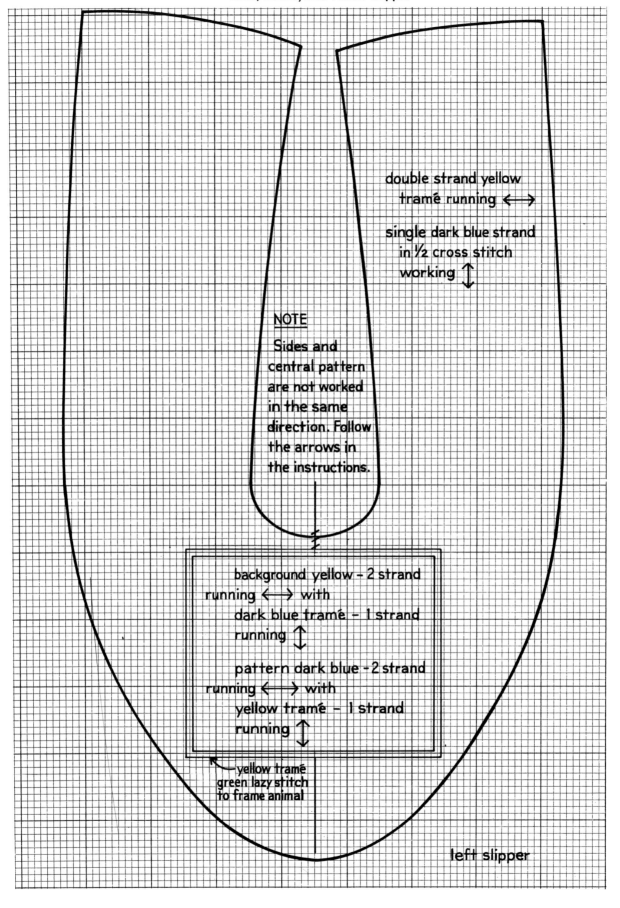

double strand yellow
tramé running ⟷

single dark blue strand
in ½ cross stitch
working ↕

NOTE
Sides and
central pattern
are not worked
in the same
direction. Follow
the arrows in
the instructions.

background yellow - 2 strand
running ⟷ with
dark blue tramé - 1 strand
running ↕

pattern dark blue - 2 strand
running ⟷ with
yellow tramé - 1 strand
running ↕

yellow tramé
green lazy stitch
to frame animal

left slipper

Checked Slipper

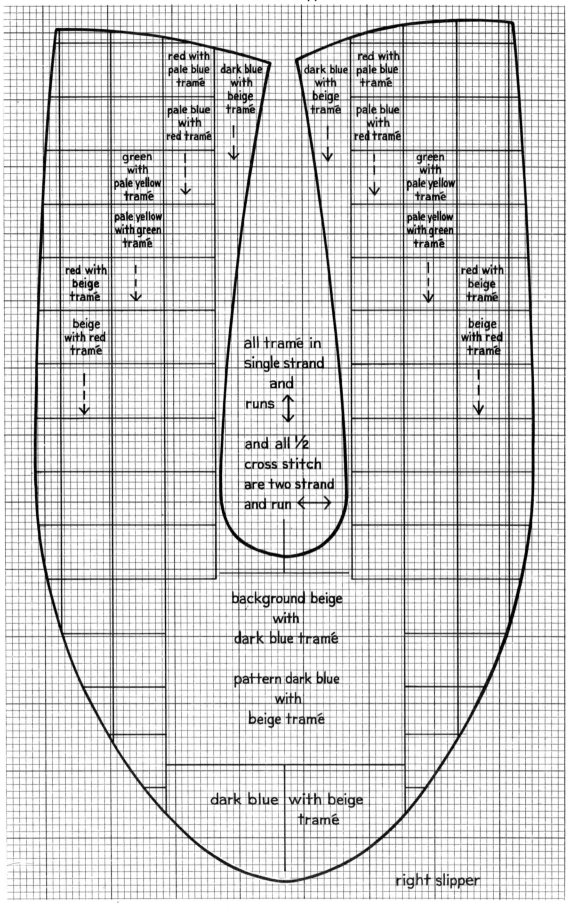

red with pale blue tramé

dark blue with beige tramé

dark blue with beige tramé

red with pale blue tramé

pale blue with red tramé

pale blue with red tramé

green with pale yellow tramé

green with pale yellow tramé

pale yellow with green tramé

pale yellow with green tramé

red with beige tramé

red with beige tramé

beige with red tramé

beige with red tramé

all tramé in single strand and runs ↕ and all ½ cross stitch are two strand and run ↔

background beige with dark blue tramé

pattern dark blue with beige tramé

dark blue with beige tramé

right slipper

Bargello Bag

10-point mono canvas

11½ inches deep

Colors: dark red—810   white—026   cherry—R 60   soft
   green—522   yellow—456   pale blue—743   dark green
   —507

3 strands of wool throughout

This colorful and very contemporary bag was woven in the compact weft twining method by the Winnebago Indians of Black Falls, Wisconsin. In this method of weaving the weft is tight and completely covers the warp. Thus, the pattern and color changes are the result of variations on the warp—just the reverse of the spaced weft method discussed in the preceding pattern.

This design is extremely flexible. Any depth can be made up by adding or subtracting patterns, and any length by continuing the patterns until you want to stop! The patterns are different sizes, so it is impossible to have the patterns blend at the seam.

Decide on the depth of the bag. Cut and tape the canvas. Starting at the top of the canvas, do the continental stitch border for the entire length you desire. This will be the guideline for all other patterns.

You will be working from left to right on this design.

Roll the canvas so about eight inches of the left side of the canvas is flat. Pin the canvas as explained on page 8. Starting at the top of the pattern and the canvas do one triangular pattern for the exposed length of the canvas, and then the next, and so on to the bottom. Roll the finished portion of the canvas and unroll another length of fresh canvas. Continue working in this fashion until you reach the end of the continental stitch border.

The stitches are varying lengths of satin stitches:

(1) the top triangular pattern—the stitches cover 2, 3, 4, 7, 4, 3, 2 threads to form the triangle;

(2) the center triangular pattern—the stitches cover 2, 3, 4, 5, 4, 3, 2 threads to form the triangle;

(3) the diamond shapes—the stitches cover 2 threads.

Bargello Bag

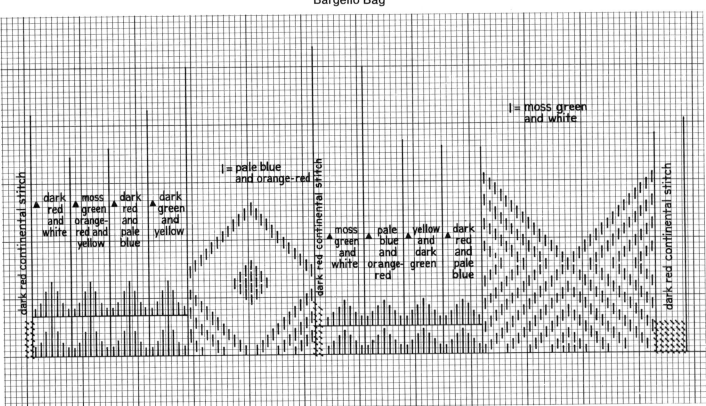

Needlecase and Eyeglass Case

18-point mono canvas
Colors: purple—640   pink—865   white
Single thread throughout

These last items you have earned! A needlecase for your gold needle and an eyeglass case for the glasses you have acquired since starting to do needlework!

These cases are examples of the floral designs so admired by the Woodland Indians. The most popular floral design was the double curve.

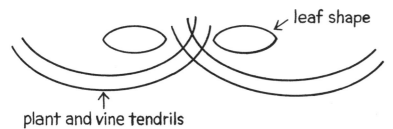

leaf shape

plant and vine tendrils

Sometimes this curve becomes so abstract that it resembles an enormous bow as seen in the eyeglass case.

The cases are done in quite a different technique. It is rather fun and can be done on almost any material. Try it, or if you prefer do the designs on canvas with a basketweave background.

The cases are done on velvet. The design is drawn on eighteen-point mono canvas which is securely pinned to a piece of velvet and the two are worked together. Be very careful to put the needle *straight* up and down through the canvas and velvet. The stitches are so tiny that unless they are stitched straight they will look like mistakes instead of complete stitches.

When the stitching is finished cautiously unravel the canvas, pulling each thread out from under the needlepoint. If a thread sticks look to see where it has been caught by a stitch, carefully cut the thread next to the snag, and then pull out the two ends of the thread. When you are finished all the needlework will be lying directly on top of the velvet.

Take the piece to the cleaner and ask him to pin it to the steaming machine and then steam it from the bottom. It should remain pinned to the machine until it is cool, to prevent any shrinkage.

The eyeglass case may have a plain velvet back or you may improvise with the abstract flower and initials as shown on the pattern.

The borders, flowers, and the floral curve are continental stitch. The large star flower is outlined in stem stitch. The smaller flowers are long straight stitches and the white blossoms are french knots.

Eyeglass case

Needlecase

Alphabet

$A\ B\ C\ D\ E\ F\ G\ H\ I\ J\ K\ L\ M\ N$

$O\ P\ Q\ R\ S\ T\ U\ V\ W\ X\ Y\ Z$

Here is your Woodland Indian design. It is taken from a fabulously colorful Potowami Indian skirt. The background is red felt and the appliqué is silk.

Potawami appliqué

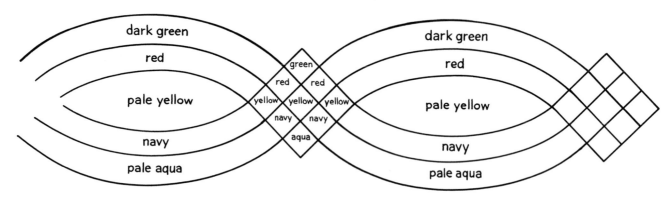

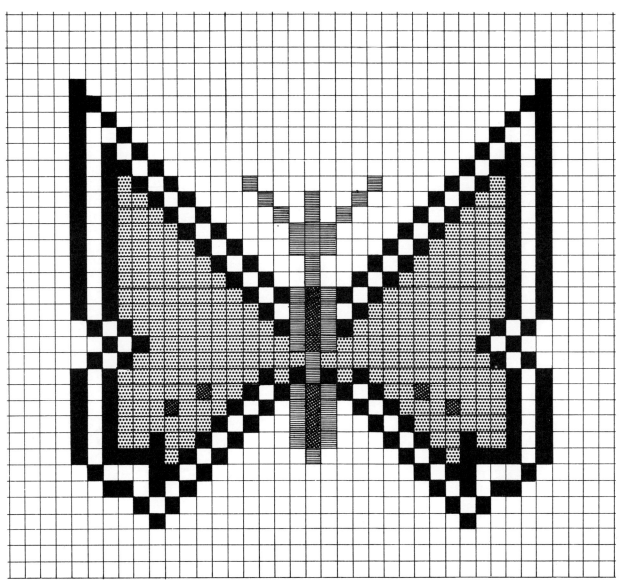

From a beaded belt, Jicarilla Apache, New Mexico

Chain stitch this is a directional stitch so start the rows at the same end of the work and always work in the same direction.

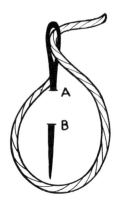

Split stitch the needle comes up through the center of the previous stitch. Shorten the stitches when rounding a corner—up at A, down at B, up at C.

Stem stitch another directional stitch. Always start at the same end of the work. Keep the thread on the same side of the work—up at A, down at B, up at C, down at D, up at B.

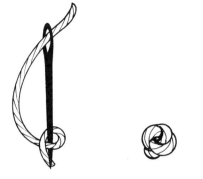

French knot bring thread up through fabric, wrap thread once around the needle, and re-enter the hole the thread came through. To make a larger knot use more threads in the needle. Do not wrap more than once around the needle.

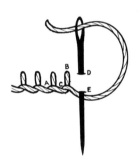

Buttonhole stitch space stitches so outside edge lies flat.

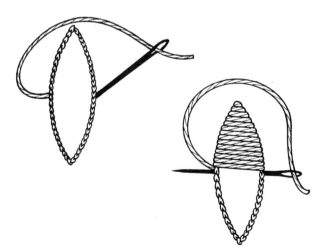

Satin stitch
(1) outline with split stitch
(2) starting at the center lay straight threads across. Work toward the end and then return to the center and finish toward the other end as shown.

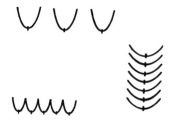

Fly stitch needle up at A, make a large loop under the needle, down at B and up at C. Tack the loop by making a small stitch to D.

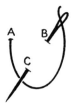

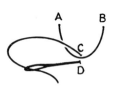

Single feather stitch—the fish hook

Seeding stitch

Back stitch similar to the seeding stitch except that the stitches touch each other.

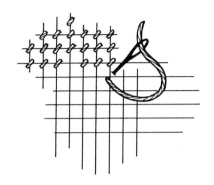

Tied laid work

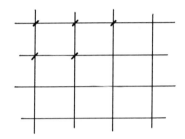

Trellis filling
(1) lay threads vertically and horizontally and tie down diagonally at each intersection

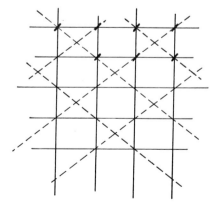

(2) lay a second set of threads diagonally over every other diagonal line and tie down horizontally at each intersection.

78

Continental stitch

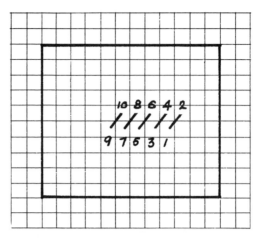

Basketweave

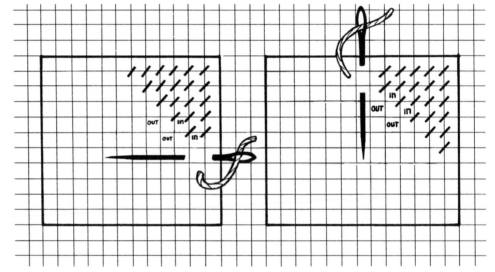

(a) upward row, needle horizontal

(b) downward row, needle vertical (Make sure not to put two of the same rows together. This will leave a mark on the finished work. Check the back of the work and start a row that will cross the stitches of the previous row.)

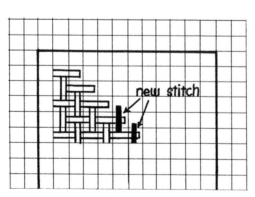

new stitch

(c) the stitches on the new row must cross the stitches of the previous row.

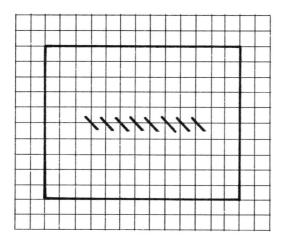

Half cross stitch this stitch is a left-handed continental stitch.

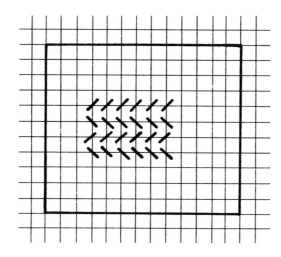

Lazy knit stitch half cross stitch and continental stitch alternating.

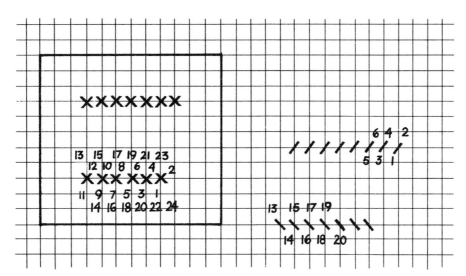

Cross stitch the easiest way to do rows of cross stitch is to do a row of continental stitch, and cover it with a row of half cross stitch.

80

Straight gobelin stitch

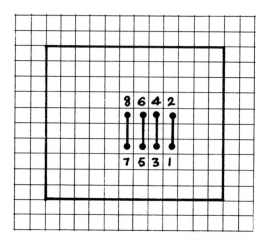

Encroaching gobelin stitch

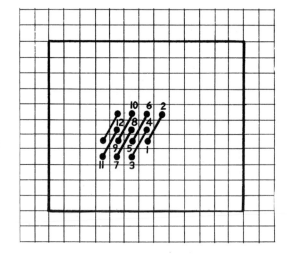

Brick stitch

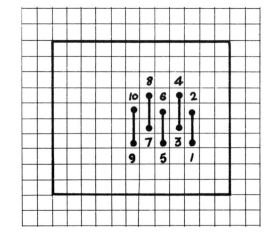

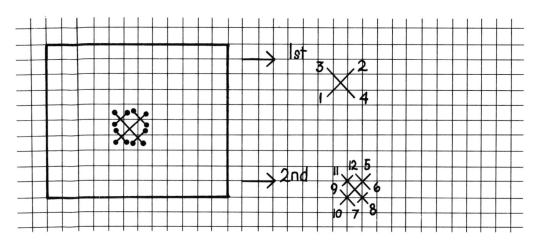

Rice stitch   (1) make a regular cross stitch   (2) cross each corner of the cross stitch

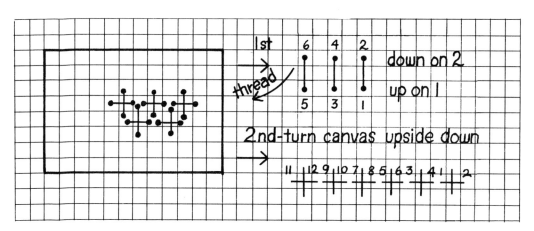

Upright cross stitch   (1) up on 1, down on 2, skip a hole, up on 3, down on 4
(2) turn the canvas upside down and do a backstitch to make the crosses.

Bump stitch

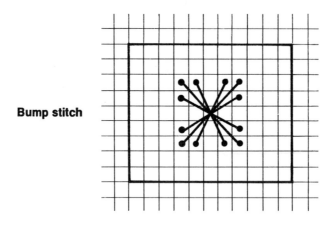

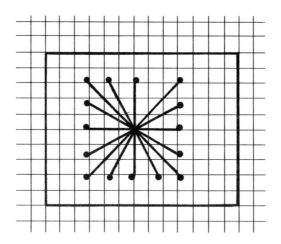

Spider web stitch one half of one spoke is omitted so there will be an uneven number of spokes. With a threaded needle, weave in and out around the spokes, pushing the thread into the center, until the entire cross is filled in.

Tassel   for a puffy mixed thread tassel:
(1) lay mixed threads flat
(2) tightly knot the threads in the middle with a separate thread
(3) bend the bundle in half
(4) wrap with a long thread and tie about three-fourths of an inch from the top
(5) trim the ends.

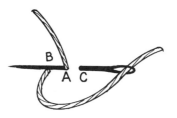

B A C D E

Turkey stitch
(1) insert the needle at A and come up at B. Make a short stitch by going down at C and up at A. This stitch is a tacking stitch and lies flat in front
(2) make a long loop stitch from A to D and come up at C. Hold this stitch with the left thumb to keep it long, and in the back
(3) tack the loop down by making a short stitch from E to D, in front of the loop
(4) make another loop stitch in the back
(5) tack it down with a short front stitch.

Bibliography

Anthropological Papers of The American Museum of Natural History, vol. 16, Alanson Skinner, Menomini Social Life and Ceremonial Bundles, 1915.

Bulletin Publication of the Museum of Milwaukee, vol. 5, no. 1, p. 35, Skinner.

Bulietin of the Journal of American Ethnology, vol. 95, p. 55, and vol. 41, pp. 364, 373, Biren Bonnerjea, Smithsonian Institute, 1963.

The Book of Indian Crafts and Indian Lore, Julian Harris Salomon, Harper & Brothers, New York and London, 1928.

The Indian How Book, Arthur C. Parker, George H. Doran Co., New York, 1927.

The North American Indians: A Sourcebook, ed. by Roger C. Owen, James J. F. Peetz, and Anthony D. Fisher, The Macmillan Co., New York, Collier-Macmillan Ltd:, London, 1967.

Introduction to American Anthropology, vol. 1: *North and Middle America,* Gordon R. Willey, Prentice-Hall Anthropology Series, Prentice-Hall Inc., Englewood Cliffs, New Jersey, 1966.

Primitive Art, Its Traditions and Styles, Paul S. Wingert, Oxford University Press, New York, 1962.

American Indian, Oliver LaFarge, Crown Publishers, Inc., New York, 1956.

Indians of the Plains, Robert H. Lowie, and *Indians of the Northwest Coast,* Philip Dricker, American Museum Science Books, Natural History Press, Doubleday and Company.

Hanley, Hope, *Needlepoint,* Charles Scribner's Sons, New York, 1963.

Sidney, Sylvia, *Needlepoint Book,* Van Nostrand Reinhold Company, New York, 1968.

Enthoven, Jacqueline, *The Stitches of Creative Embroidery,* Van Nostrand Reinhold Company, New York, 1964.

Wilson, Erica, *Crewel Embroidery,* Charles Scribner's Sons, New York, 1962.